Springtime Activities
for the Early Years

Val Edgar

Brilliant Publications

Introduction

This pre-school book has been written to provide a bank of fun ideas and activities to use at springtime and Easter with children aged 3–5 years.

The book is made up of photocopiable sheets focusing on communication, language and literacy, mathematical development and creative development.

Each worksheet is supported by activity suggestions linked to the DfES *Curriculum Guidance for the Foundation Stage* (Qualifications and Curriculum Authority, 2000). The suggestions are clearly coded to show which area of the curriculum is covered by each activity:
- Personal, social and emotional development (PSE)
- Communication, language and literacy (CLL)
- Mathematical development (MD)
- Knowledge and understanding of the world (KUW)
- Physical development (PD)
- Creative development (CD)

Publisher's information

Brilliant Publications
1 Church View
Sparrow Hall Farm
Edlesborough, Dunstable
Bedfordshire LU6 2ES

Tel: 01525 229720
Fax: 01525 229725
E-mail: sales@brilliantpublications.co.uk
Website: www.brilliantpublications.co.uk

Written and illustrated by Val Edgar

Printed in Malta by Interprint
First published in 2004
10 9 8 7 6 5 4 3 2 1

© Val Edgar 2004

ISBN 1 903 853 591

The right of Val Edgar to be identified as the author of this work has been asserted by her in accordance with the Copyright, Designs and Patents Act 1988.

Pages 9–48 may be photocopied by individual teachers for class use, without permission from the publisher. The materials may not be reproduced in any other form or for any other purpose without the prior permission of the publisher.

Contents

Activity suggestions 4

Communication, language and literacy
Spring babies 9
Ducklings 10
Dotty Easter egg 11
The bumble bee 12
Letter c 13
Letter d 14
Letter s 15
Letter g 16
Bunny's maze 17
Come to the party 18
Patterns 19
Happy families 20
Spring cleaning 21
Tadpoles and frogs 22
Caterpillars and butterflies 23
Seeds and sunflowers 24
Spinner game 25

Mathematical development
Odd-one-out 26
Colour and count 27
Dot-to-dot 28
Yellow 29
Match the bonnets 30
Easter egg colours 31
How many? 32
Daffodils 33
Caterpillar pieces 34
Washing line 35
Rolling eggs 36
Bunny 37
Tadpoles 38
Butterfly jigsaw 39
Crazy caterpillars 40

Creative development
Blossom card 41
Mother's day 42
My Easter bonnet 43
Easter card 44
April showers 45
Easter egg basket 46
Petal prints 47
Colour-mix caterpillar 48

Activity suggestions

This section explains how to use those sheets marked "see notes", and also provides extra activity ideas to accompany each worksheet. Each activity is coded to show the curricular area it covers (please refer to the introduction).

Spring babies (page 9)
❖ Play **Animal noises** – half the children are each given a card with a mother animal written or drawn on it, the other half have the baby animals. By walking around making the appropriate animal noises the children match themselves into mother/baby pairs without showing their cards or speaking. **(KUW, CLL)**

Ducklings (page 10)
❖ Take a trip to your local park to watch ducklings, or watch a video. **(KUW)**
❖ Waddle like ducklings following mother duck. **(PD)**
❖ Read *The Ugly Duckling*. **(CLL)**

Dotty Easter egg (page 11)
❖ Draw a large egg shape in damp sand. Let the children use fingers or tools to decorate it with patterns. **(CLL, CD)**

The bumble bee (page 12)
❖ Make bumble bee puppets using old stockings stuffed with newspaper and painted in stripes. **(CD)** Hang by thread and let the children take them to 'visit' all the flowers, buzzing loudly. **(KUW)**

Letter c, Letter d, Letter s, Letter g (pages 13–16)
❖ Make up more alliterative phrases. **(CLL)**
❖ Use pipe cleaners to make the letters. **(CLL)** Then go on to make pipe cleaner flowers. **(CD)**

Bunny's maze (page 17)
❖ Hide some Easter eggs then give the children instructions to find them – turn left, over, under, behind etc. **(CLL)** Let the children give each other instructions. **(PSE)**
❖ Have an Easter egg hunt in the garden. Encourage sharing of all the treasure. **(PSE)**

Come to the party (page 18)
❖ Have an Easter party: make a guest list, make a shopping list. **(CLL)**
❖ Take a trip to the local shop and prepare snacks. **(KUW)**

- ❖ Have an Easter bonnet competition, with prizes for the biggest, most colourful, most unusual etc. **(CD)**
- ❖ Play **Easter egg skittles**. Roll Easter eggs to knock over a toy bunny. **(PD)**

Patterns (page 19)
- ❖ Have an Easter picnic with only yellow and green food – egg and cress sandwiches, apples, lemon tarts etc. **(KUW)**

Happy families (page 20)
- ❖ Discuss families in springtime. **(KUW)**
- ❖ Arrange a visit to a farm park. Look and listen for the babies. Do they sound different from the adult animals? **(KUW)**

Spring cleaning (page 21)
- ❖ Look around carefully then discuss what needs cleaning. Each child should have a responsibility, however small. **(PSE)**

Tadpoles and frogs (page 22)
- ❖ Colour the pictures on the sheet. Then cut out the six parts and punch holes at top of each. Use two lengths of wool or thread to join the pages to make a book in which the pages can be flipped over indefinitely. This should help to show the idea of a life cycle continuing generation after generation. **(KUW, CLL)**
- ❖ Role-play – lie curled up, uncurl, wriggle, extend legs, begin to walk, jump. **(PD)**

Caterpillars and butterflies (page 23)
- ❖ Make a book as above. **(KUW, CLL)** Role-play as appropriate. **(PD)**

Seeds and sunflowers (page 24)
- ❖ Make a book as above. **(KUW, CLL)** Role-play as appropriate. **(PD)**
- ❖ Grow sunflower seeds. Begin by placing them between two damp sheets of kitchen paper. Check and observe every day. After a few days the seeds will open and the shoot and root will begin to grow. Have the children look, discuss, draw, photograph. At this stage plant out in the garden. **(KUW)**
- ❖ Go on a 'bud and shoot hunt' in the local park. Go back a week later, then a fortnight later, to see the changes. **(KUW)**

Spinner game (page 25)
- ❖ Play **Spinner.** Cut out the spinner and push a pencil through the centre circle for it to spin on. Have the children sit in a small circle. When the spinner stops the children all do the action shown, eg wriggling across the floor like a tadpole. **(CLL, PD)**

- Have an Easter sports day – Easter bonnet hat race, egg and spoon, Easter bunny hopping relay. **(PD)**

Odd-one-out (page 26)
- Read *The Ugly Duckling* and discuss the importance of feeling part of a family. **(PSE)**

Colour and count (page 27)
- Sit and watch a flower bed. How many minibeasts visit it over ten minutes? What are they? Are they living there, pollinating, eating? **(KUW, CLL)**

Dot-to-dot (page 28)
- Think of a name for the tadpole. Help the children think of a great adventure for him. Retell the children's story and get them to illustrate it to make a book about his adventure. **(CLL, CD)**

Yellow (page 29)
- Make a collection of yellow things. **(MD)**
- Play **Kim's game**. Take ten of the yellow objects. Show them, remove one, and see if the children can tell which one has gone. **(MD)**

Match the bonnets (page 30)
- Have the children describe each bonnet in detail. **(CLL, MD)**

Easter egg colours (page 31)
- Play **Boiled egg bowls**. Colour one hard-boiled egg black and roll it on flat grass. The children then roll their own brightly painted eggs to see who can get closest. **(PD, PSE)**

How many? (page 32)
- Set up a large spring picture with a tree, pond and field. Add frogspawn, tadpoles, blossom, spring flowers etc. as the children learn about them. Change the picture as the children see nature changing outside. **(KUW, CD)**

Daffodils (page 33)
- Look at different varieties of daffodil. Discuss the various colours, sizes and shapes. **(KUW)** Let a child describe one variety to the others and see if they can pick it out. **(CLL, MD)**

Caterpillar pieces (page 34)
- Play **Caterpillars**. The children run around. When you shout out a number the

children form into a line of that number of children, with their hands on the waist in front and the leader with hands up like a caterpillar's feelers. They walk around slowly in their caterpillar line until another number is called. **(PD, MD)**

Washing line (page 35)
- Make a washing line. The children bring in one of their own socks. Discuss and compare sizes, colours, patterns. **(MD)**
- Play **Odd-one-out**. The children have a pile of socks which all match into pairs except one. They have to find which is the odd-one-out as quickly as they can by matching the others. **(MD)**

Rolling eggs (page 36)
- Let the children try rolling various shapes down a slope, predicting which will roll or slide. **(MD)**
- Take the children to a slope of grass and let them find ways to come down the hill themselves – rolling on their sides, running, on their bottoms. **(PD)**

Bunny (page 37)
- Draw half a butterfly in damp sand. Let the children complete it. **(MD)**

Tadpoles (page 38)
- Try to think of a name for each tadpole, all the names starting with T. **(CLL)**

Butterfly jigsaw (page 39)
- Photocopy on card. Colour first before the jigsaw shapes are cut out. **(MD)**

Crazy caterpillars (page 40)
- Look at all the caterpillars and have the children select a favourite and explain why. Describe the catarpillars' moods and discuss why a caterpillar might be sad, happy, angry. **(PSE)**

Blossom card (page 41)
- Photocopy on card. Let the children colour the picture. Then stick pink and white tissue paper, scrunched up in balls, to make blossom on the tree. **(CD)**

Mother's day (page 42)
- Photocopy on card. Let the children draw mum, gran or auntie in the middle. Decorate the frame with scrunched tissue or bright fabric scraps to make a picture present. **(CD)**

My Easter bonnet (page 43)
- Set up a hairdresser's corner. The children can experiment with hairstyles and hats for a special Easter party. **(PSE)**

Easter card (page 44)
- Photocopy on card. Colour and cut out the butterfly and the card. Stick or staple the butterfly to the inside of the card, while the card is partly closed, so that the wings flap when the card opens and shuts. **(CD)**

April showers (page 45)
- Colour the umbrellas completely with wax crayon, leaving no white spaces. Using watery blue paint, paint a thick, watery line across the top of the sheet. Hold the sheet up and the paint will run down. It will not run, however, over the waterproof wax umbrellas but will run off at the sides, keeping the children in the picture dry. **(CD, KUW)**
- Keep a note of the spring weather every day, seeing how much it can change. Discuss clothing needed when it is rainy, frosty, windy. **(KUW)**
- Go 'puddle-splashing' on an April-shower day. **(PD)**

Easter egg basket (page 46)
- Photocopy on card. Cut out two of template A, and one each of templates B and C. Colour or decorate. Stick the templates together using the tabs, as shown in the diagram. Give the basket filled with little chocolate eggs or tissue paper flowers as an Easter or Mother's day present. **(CD)**

Petal prints (page 47)
- Using fingers or potato shapes, print petals for the flowers in bright spring colours. **(CD)**

Colour-mix caterpillar (page 48)
- Use blue, yellow and white paint to mix lots of shades of green to colour each section of the caterpillar. Try to make each one different. Or stick on different greens cut from magazine pictures. **(CD)**

Spring babies

Draw lines to help the babies find their mums.

Ducklings

Help the little ducklings find mummy duck.

Dotty Easter egg

© Val Edgar
This page may be photocopied for use by the purchasing institution only.

The bumble bee

(see notes)

In spring we see

the bumble bee.

He _____

and he_____ ,

the busy little bumble bee.

by _____

Letter c

Crawling caterpillars crunching cabbages.

Colour all the **c** words.

c c c c c

cat cat cat

Letter d

Daffodils dancing over daisies.

Colour all the **d** words.

d d d d d

dog dog dog

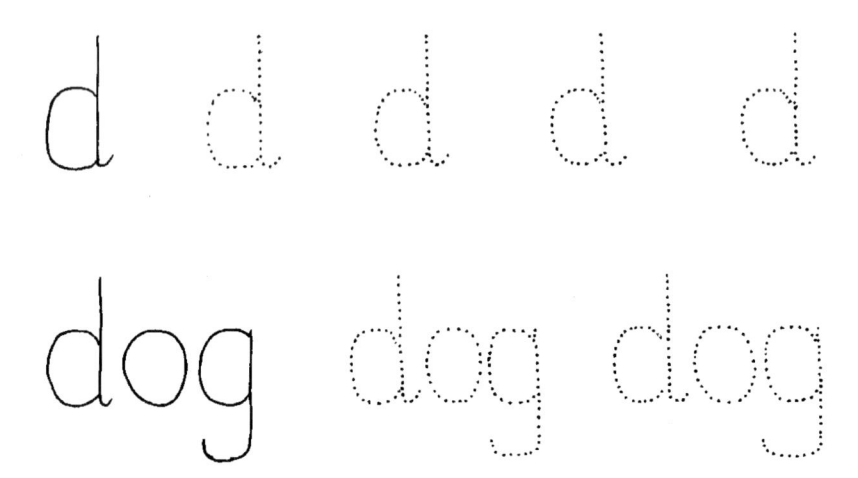

Letter S

Sunflowers swaying in the scorching sunshine.

Colour all the **S** words.

S s s s s

sun sun sun

Letter g

A goat grazing in the green grass.

Colour all the **g** words.

g g g g g

girl girl girl

Bunny's maze

Help the Easter bunny find his way to the Easter eggs.

© Val Edgar
This page may be photocopied for use by the purchasing institution only.
Springtime Activities for the Early Years
Brilliant Publications

Come to the party

Dear _____

Come to our Easter party on _____

Please wear _____

Please bring _____

With love from _____

Patterns

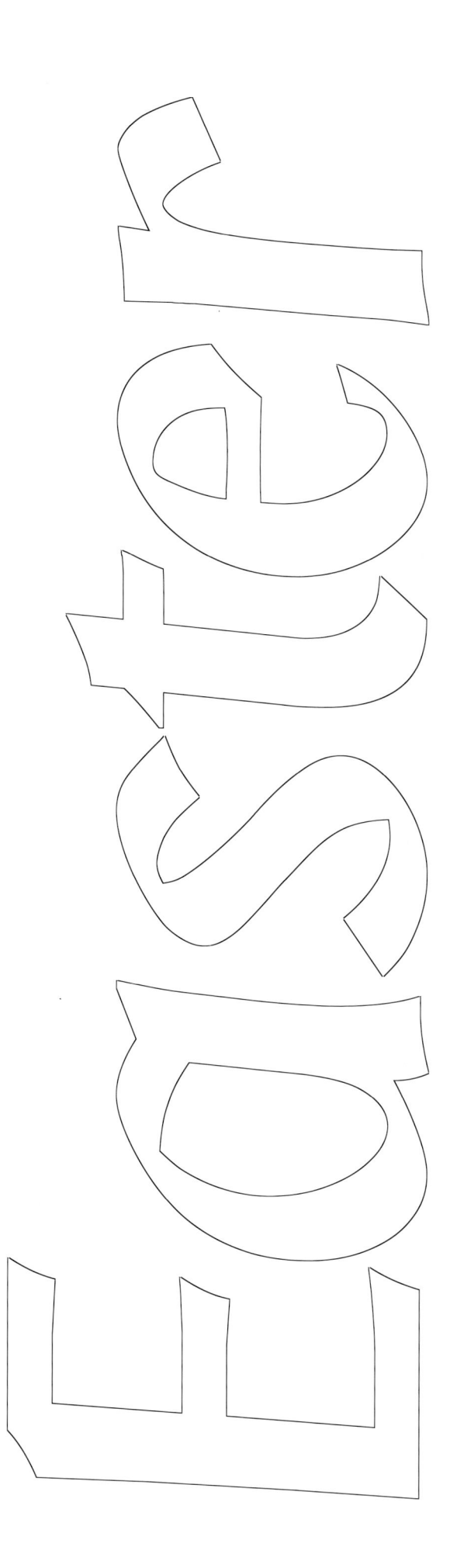

Decorate the word using yellow and green patterns.

Easter

Happy families

Talk about all the families in this spring picture.

Spring cleaning

which job?	who's doing it?	it's done! (✓)
tidying		
washing		
sweeping		
polishing		
more?		

Tadpoles and frogs

(see notes)

The frog lays eggs in the water. This is called frogspawn.

Little tadpoles hatch from the eggs. They swim like fish.

Each little tadpole starts to grow back legs.

It grows front legs and its tail gets shorter and shorter.

It can now climb out of the water and breathe air.

It's a frog.

Caterpillars and butterflies

(see notes)

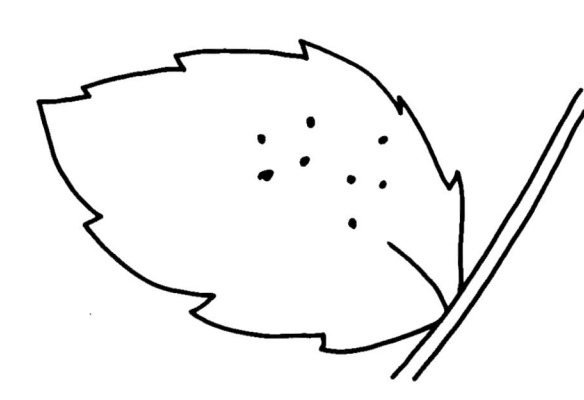

The butterfly lays eggs on a tasty leaf.

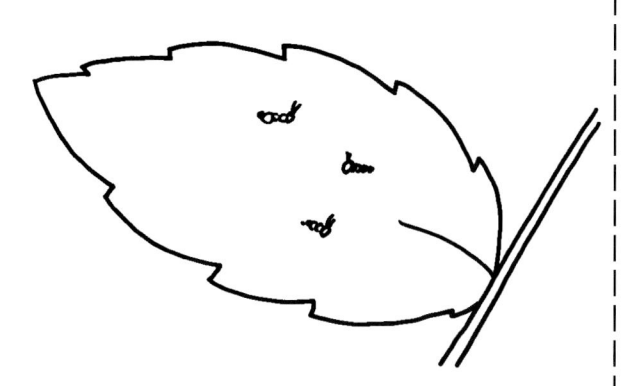

Each egg hatches into a tiny caterpillar

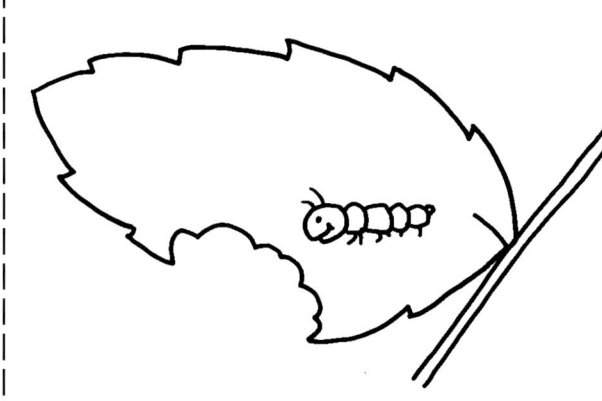

The caterpillar eats and eats until it could burst.

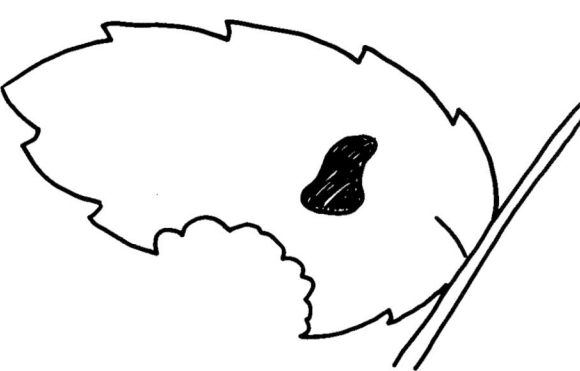

It then becomes a chrysalis with a hard shell.

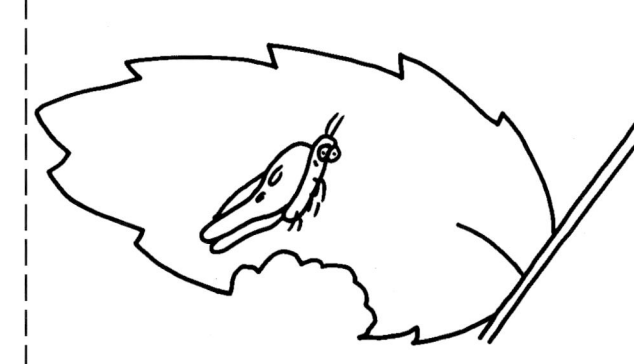

It has a rest for a while. Then it breaks out of its shell.

It's a butterfly.

Seeds and sunflowers

(see notes)

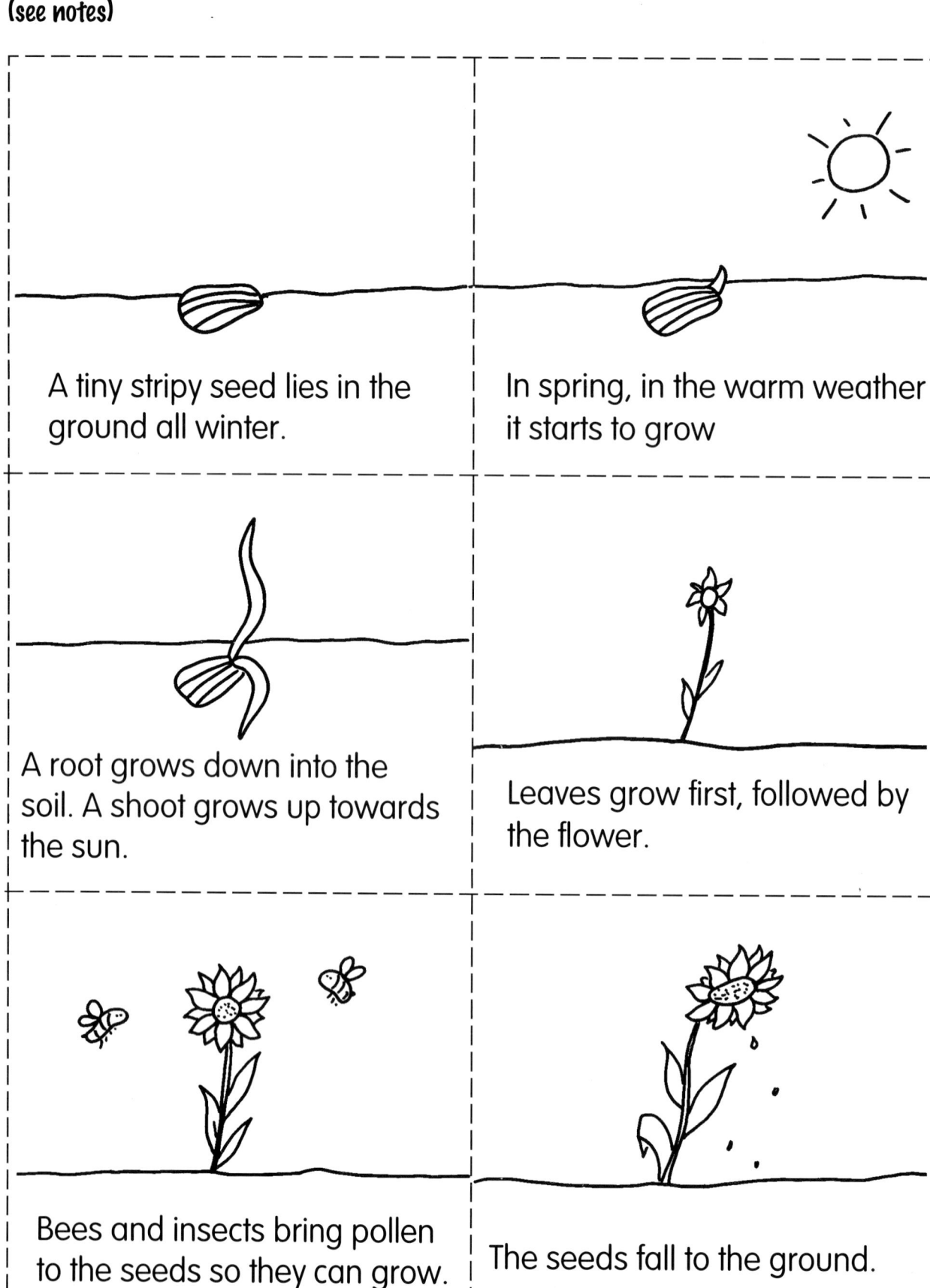

A tiny stripy seed lies in the ground all winter.

In spring, in the warm weather it starts to grow

A root grows down into the soil. A shoot grows up towards the sun.

Leaves grow first, followed by the flower.

Bees and insects bring pollen to the seeds so they can grow.

The seeds fall to the ground.

Spinner game

(see notes)

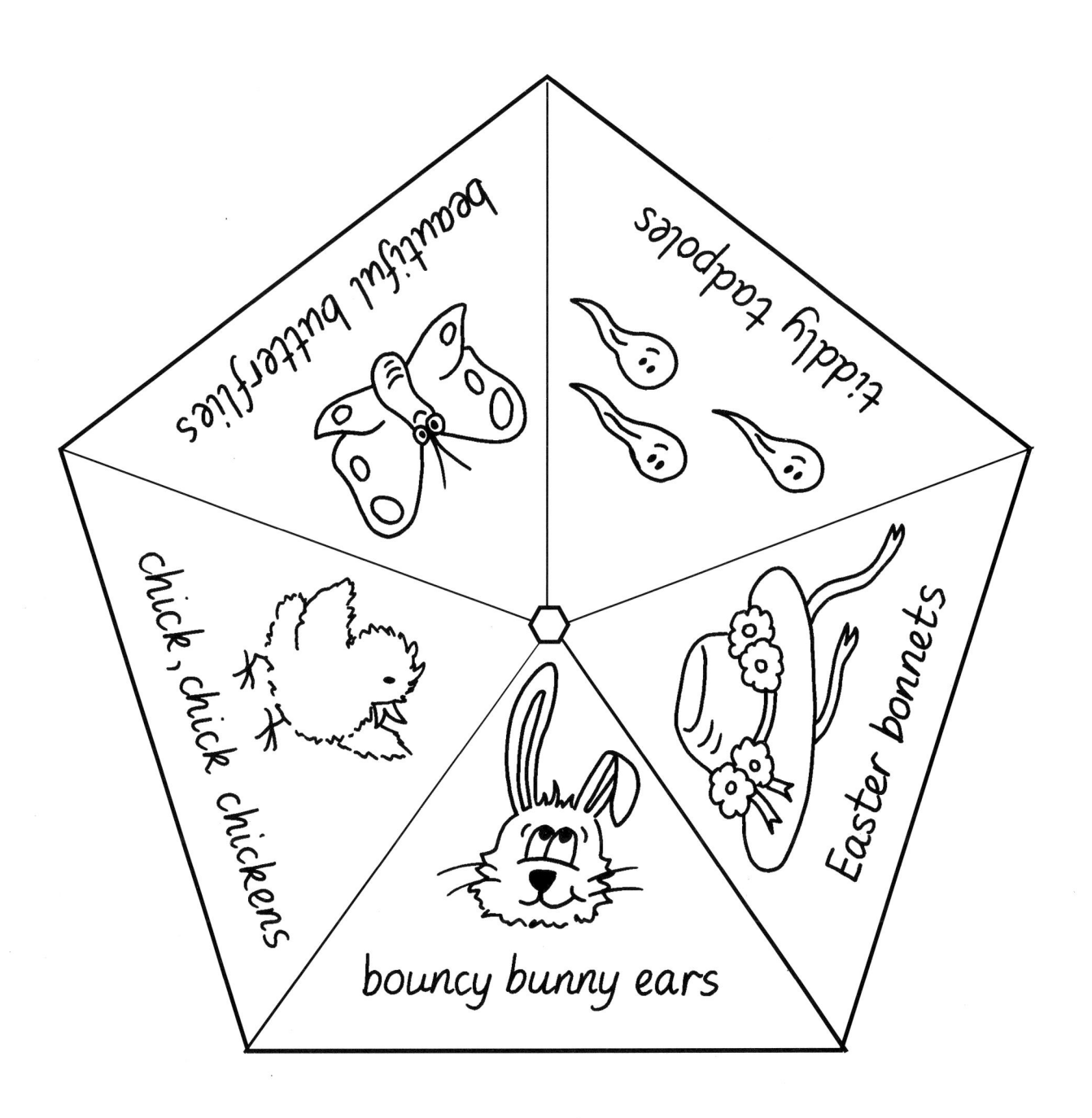

- beautiful butterflies
- tiddly tadpoles
- Easter bonnets
- bouncy bunny ears
- chick, chick chickens

© Val Edgar
Springtime Activities for the Early Years
This page may be photocopied for use by the purchasing institution only.
Brilliant Publications

Odd-one-out

Colour the odd-one-out in each row.

Colour and count

1   2   3   4   5

How many flowers? ☐

Dot-to-dot

Who is swimming in the pond?

28
Brilliant Publications
Springtime Activities for the Early Years
© Val Edgar
This page may be photocopied for use by the purchasing institution only.

Yellow

Colour all the yellow things in this spring picture.

© Val Edgar
This page may be photocopied for use by the purchasing institution only.

Springtime Activities for the Early Years

Brilliant Publications

Match the bonnets

Easter egg colours

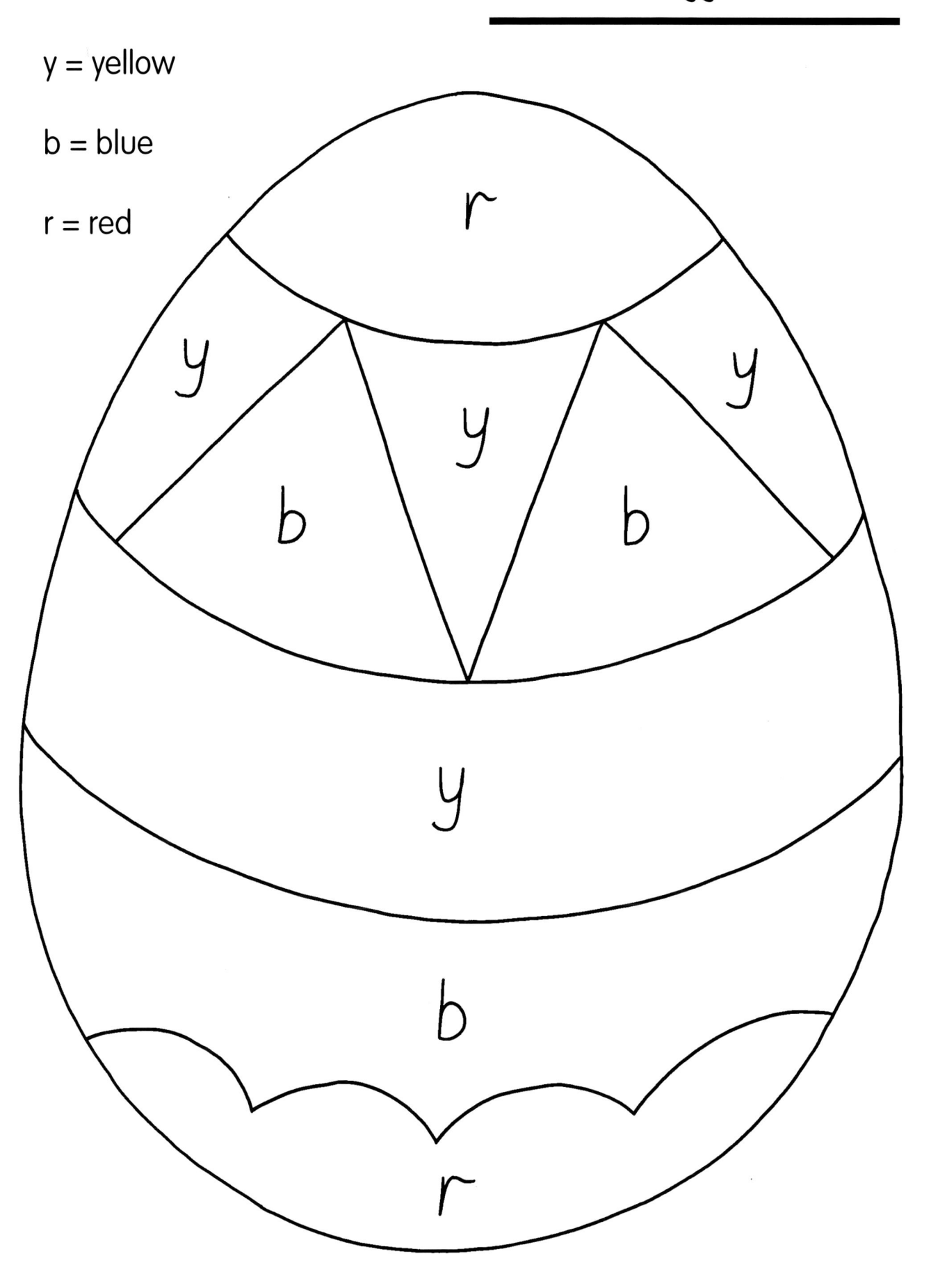

y = yellow

b = blue

r = red

How many?

1 2 3 4 5

How many?

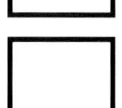

🦋 butterflies ☐   🐑 lambs ☐

🌼 daffodils ☐   🦆 ducks ☐

🐛 tadpoles ☐   🐛 caterpillars ☐

Daffodils

Draw one more daffodil under the tree.

1 2 3 4 5 6 7 8 9 10

How many daffodils? ☐

Caterpillar pieces

Cut along the lines. Put the caterpillar together in the right order.

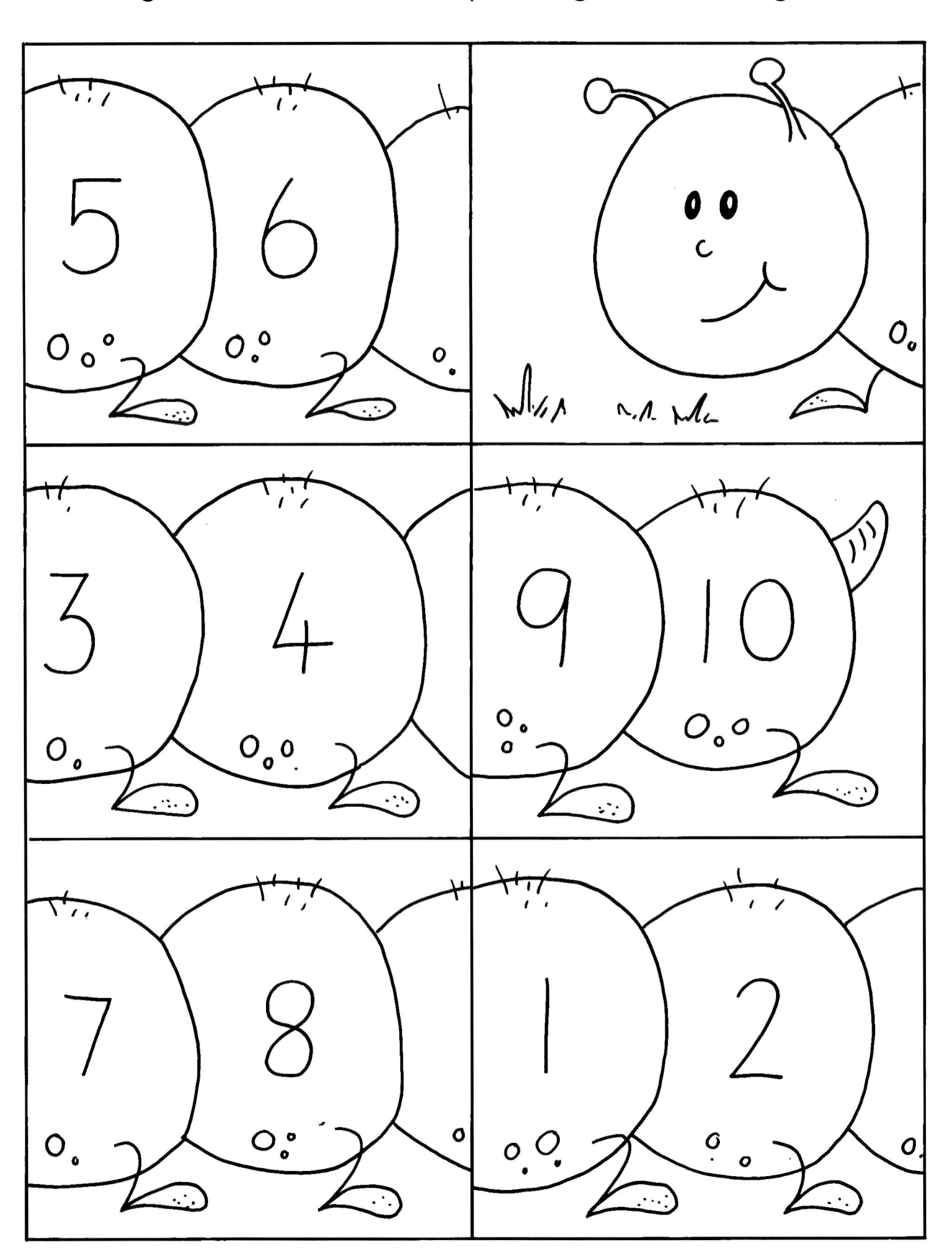

Washing line

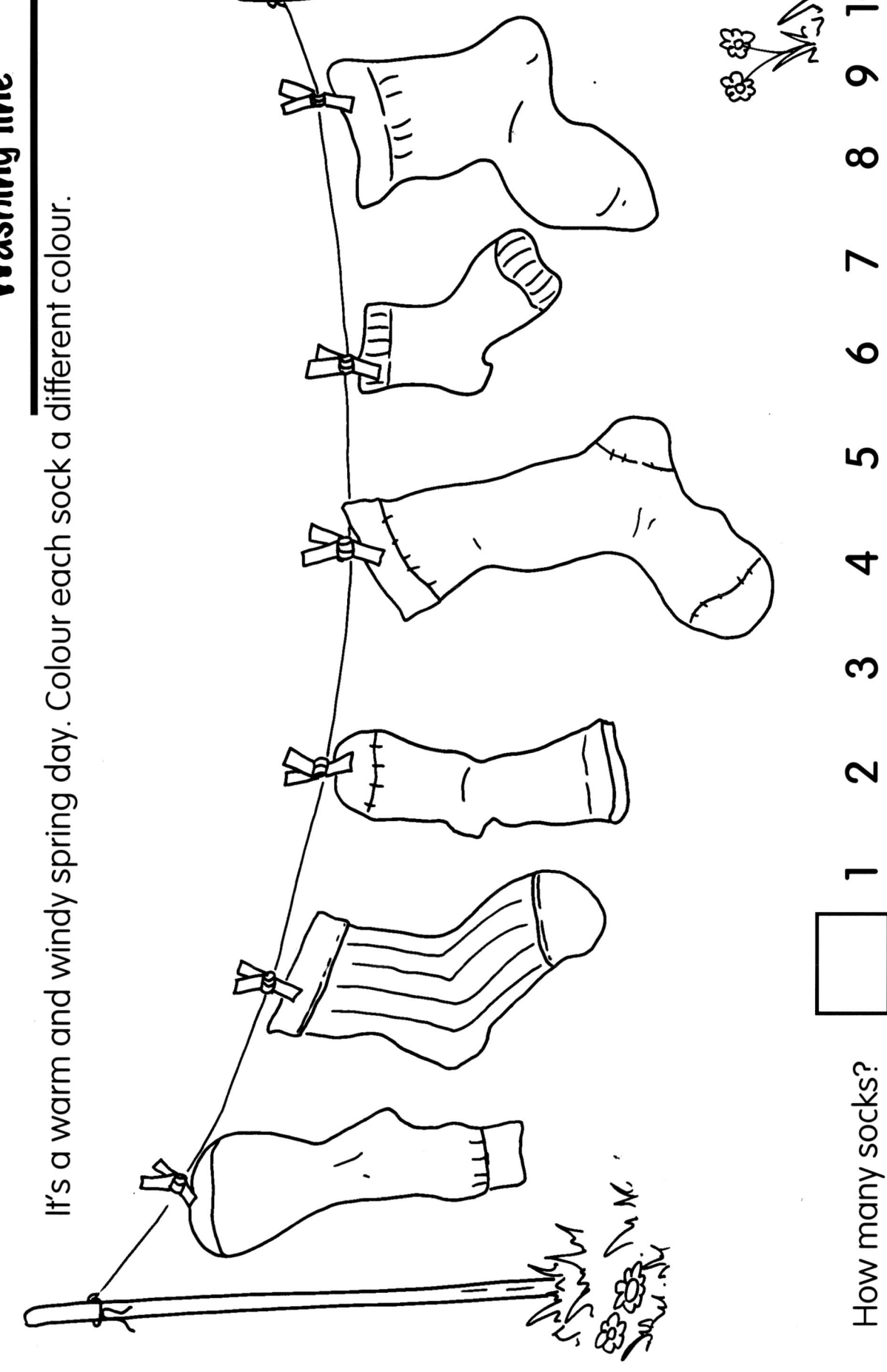

It's a warm and windy spring day. Colour each sock a different colour.

1　2　3　4　5　6　7　8　9　10

How many socks?

© Val Edgar

Springtime Activities for the Early Years

This page may be photocopied for use by the purchasing institution only.

Brilliant Publications

Rolling eggs

The Easter bunny is rolling his eggs and other shapes down the hill. Which of his shapes will roll? Colour them in.

Bunny

Draw the missing half of the Easter bunny.

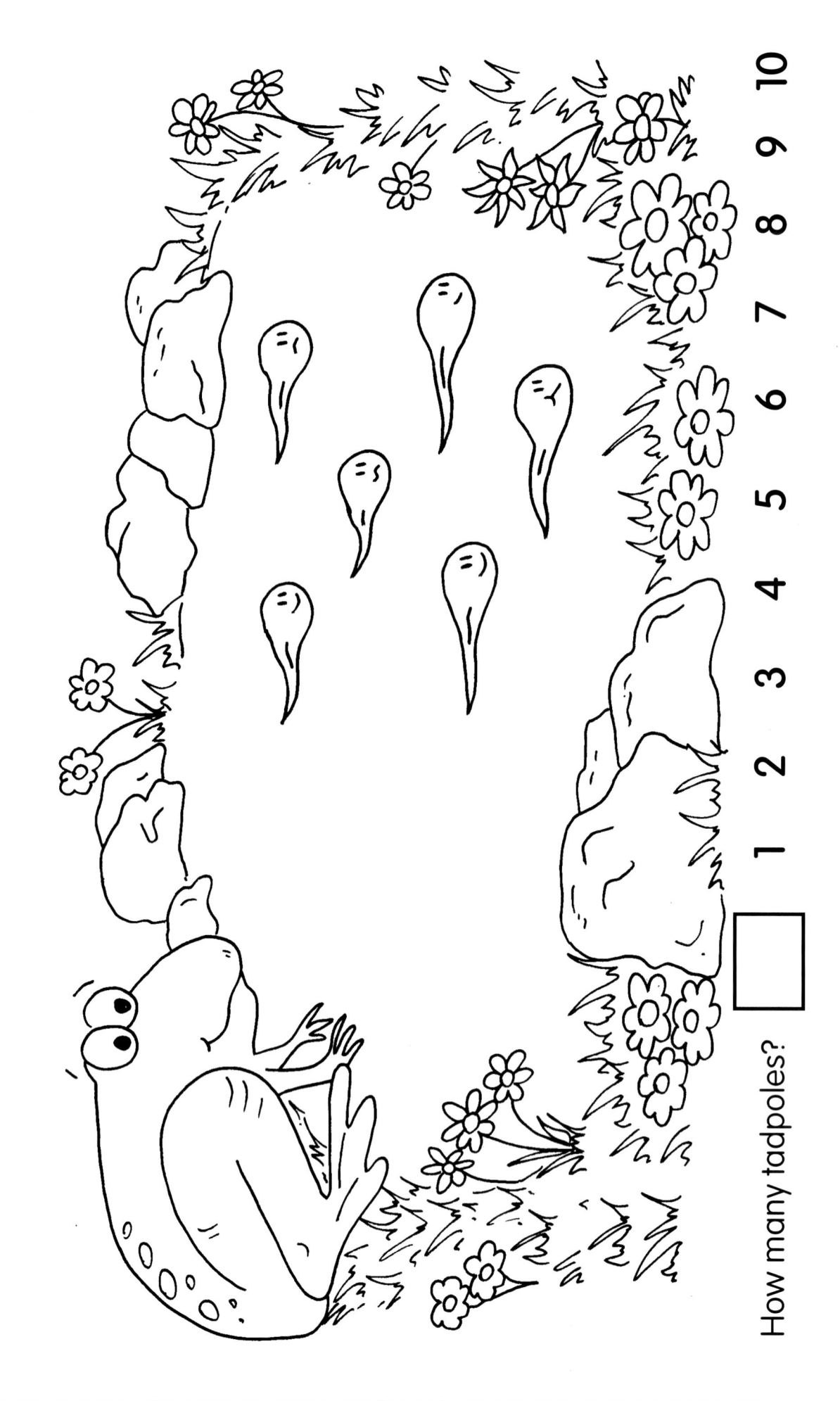

Tadpoles

Draw one more tadpole.

How many tadpoles? 1 2 3 4 5 6 7 8 9 10

Butterfly jigsaw

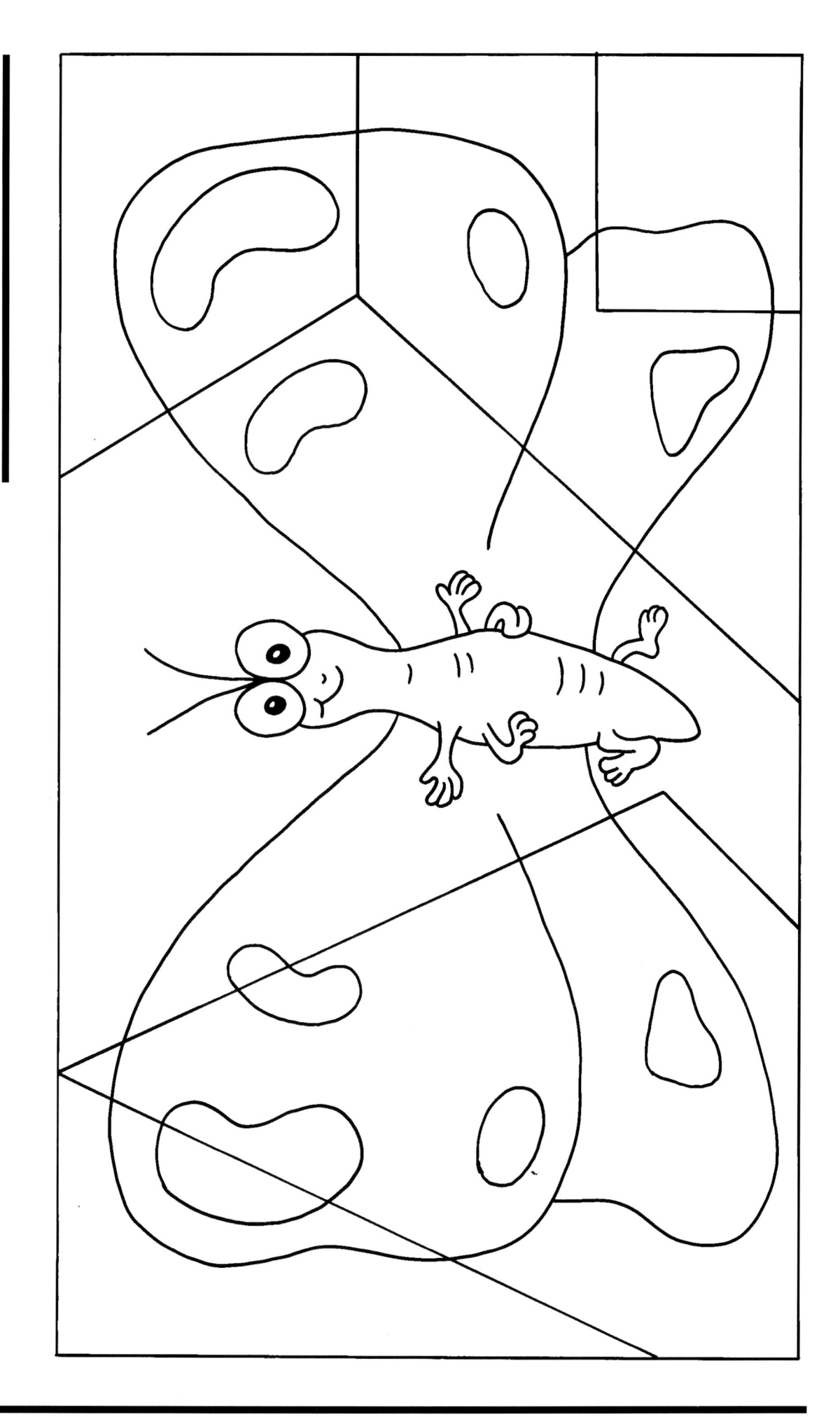

© Val Edgar

Springtime Activities for the Early Years

This page may be photocopied for use by the purchasing institution only.

39

Brilliant Publications

Crazy caterpillars

Cut out the caterpillars. Put them in order with the shortest first.

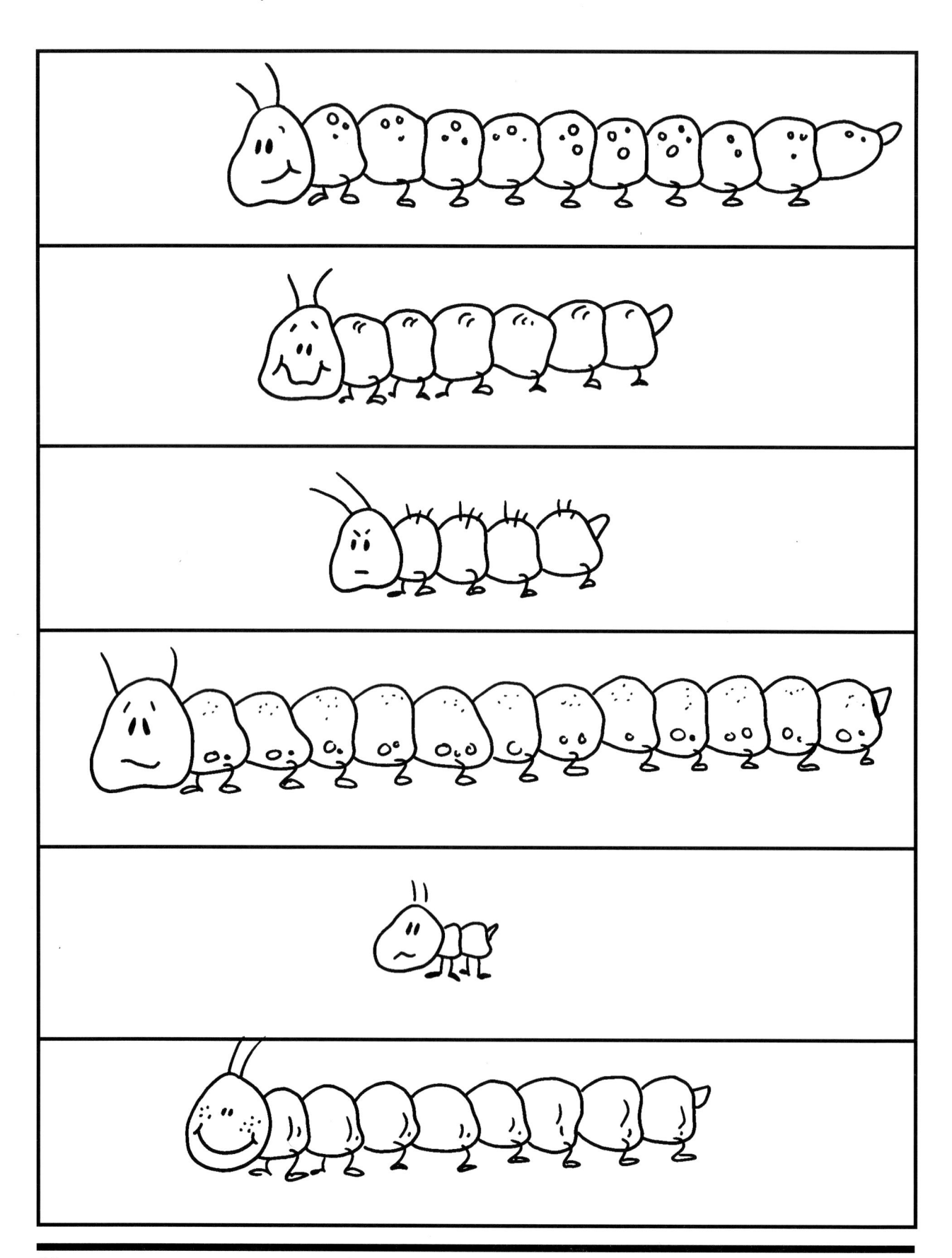

40
Brilliant Publications

Springtime Activities for the Early Years

© Val Edgar
This page may be photocopied for use by the purchasing institution only.

Blossom card

(see notes)

Happy Mother's Day

Mother's Day

(see notes)

I love ...

my _ _ _ _ _ _ _ _ _ _ _ _

My Easter bonnet

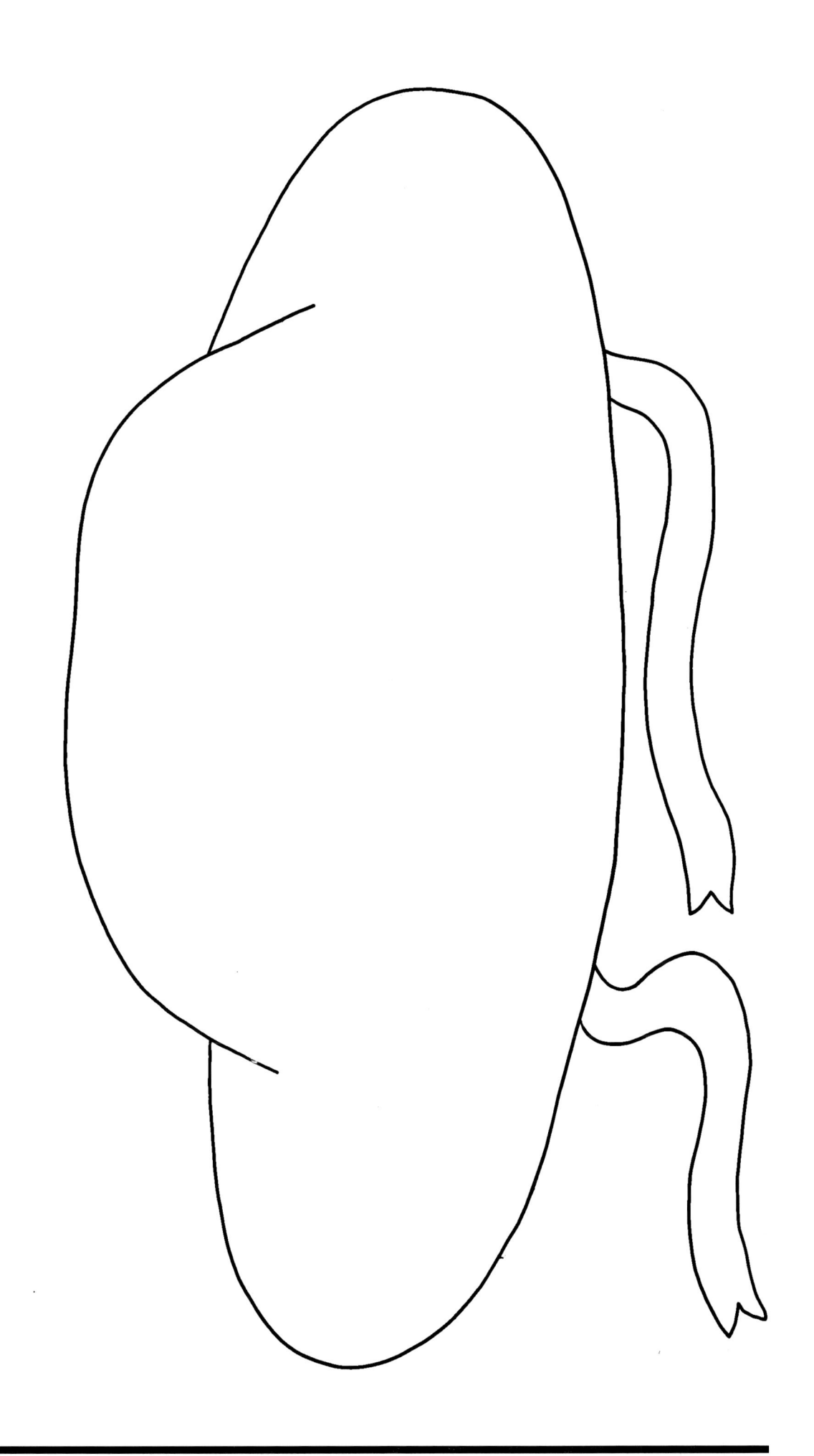

Decorate the Easter bonnet with fruit and flowers.

Easter card

(see notes)

April showers

(see notes)

Easter egg basket

(see notes)

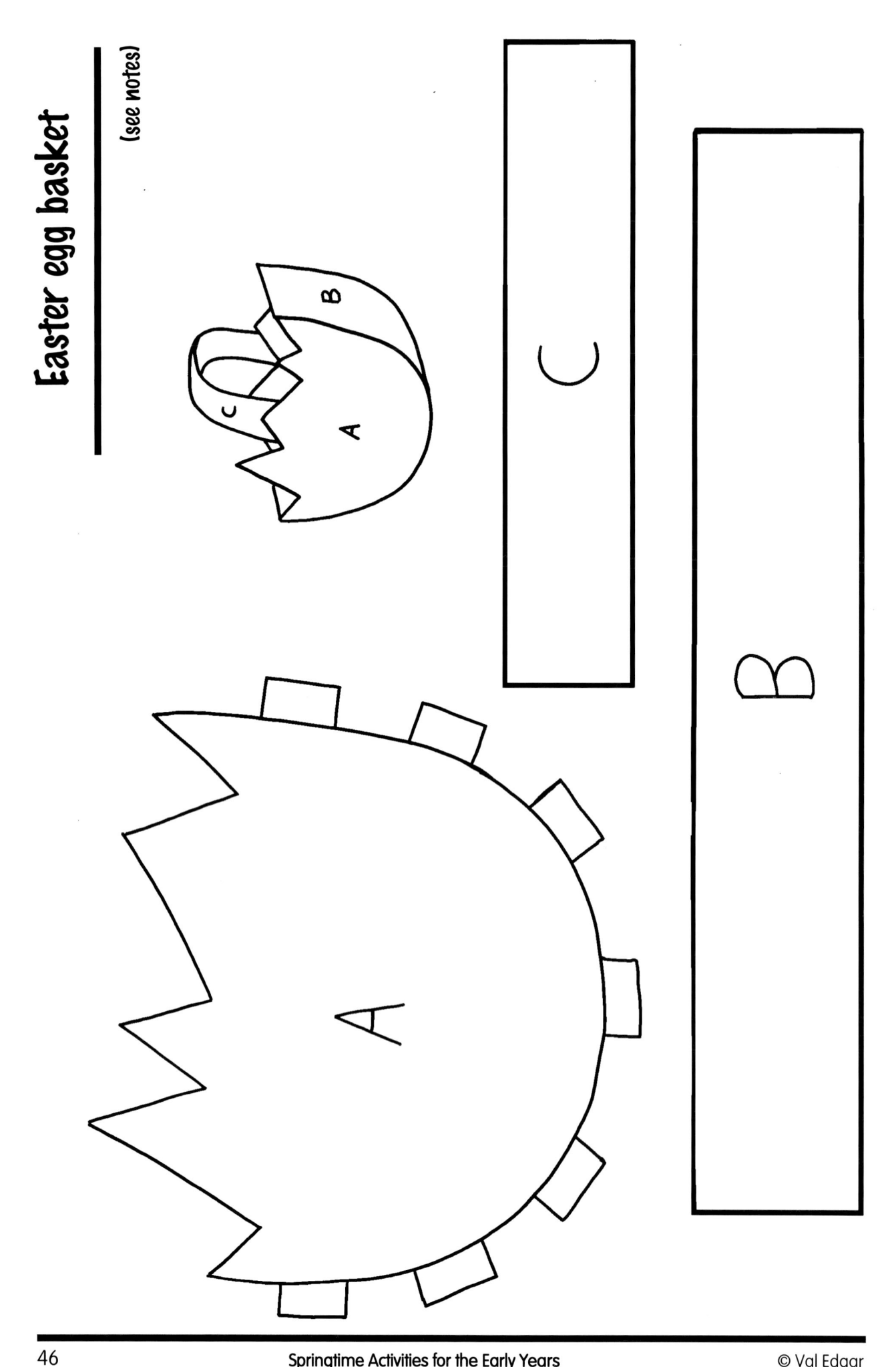

Petal prints

(see notes)

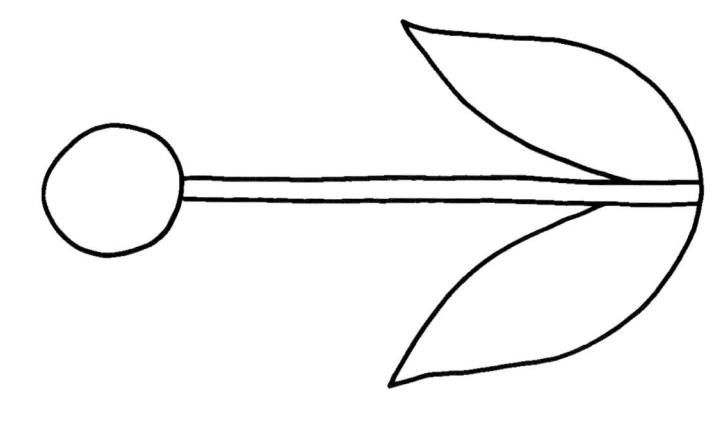

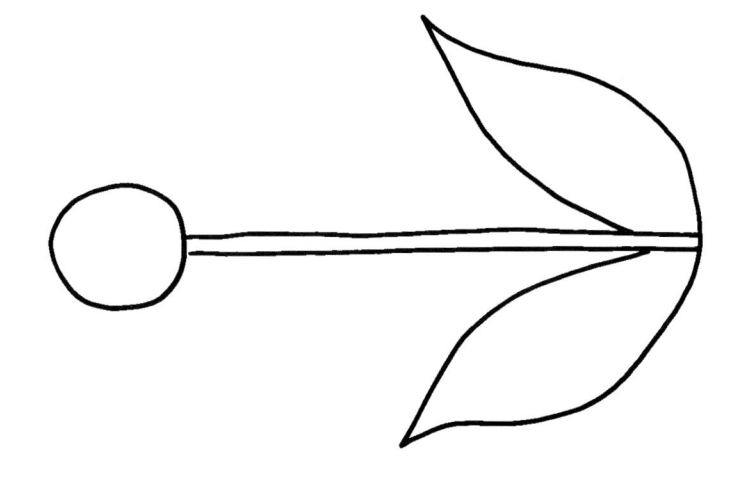

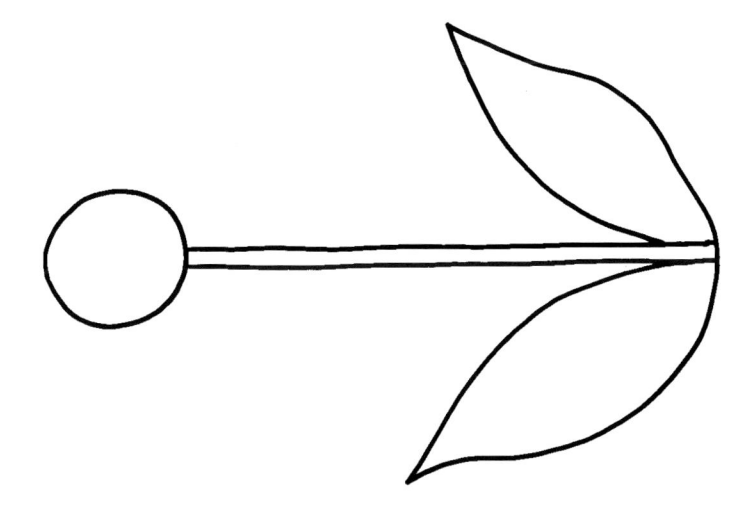

Colour-mix caterpillar (see notes)

48
Brilliant Publications

Springtime Activities for the Early Years

© Val Edgar
This page may be photocopied for use by the purchasing institution only.